History's Most Beautiful Women:

How Beauty Is Defined By ages

speedy Publishing LLC
40 e. Main st. #1156
newark, De 19711
www.speedypublishing.com

Copyright 2018

all Rights reserved. no part of this book may be reproduced or used in any way or form or by any means whether electronic or mechanical, this means that you cannot record or photocopy any material ideas or tips that are provided in this book

Beauty is the quality of being pleasing, especially to look at, or someone or something that gives great pleasure, especially when looking at it.

Nefertiti

was an Egyptian queen and the Great Royal Wife of Akhenaten, an Egyptian Pharaoh. With her husband, she reigned at what was arguably the wealthiest period of Ancient Egyptian history.

Helen of Troy

was a woman of such beauty that nations went to war over the right to call her theirs. Helen was sought after by as many as 45 of the most powerful names in the ancient Mediterranean world.

Cleopatra

was the last active pharaoh of Ptolemaic Egypt. Cleopatra was a member of the Ptolemaic dynasty, a family of Macedonian Greek origin that ruled Egypt.

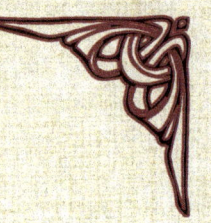

Queen of Sheba

is a queen regnant who appears in the Bible. The Queen of Sheba gained her throne with her beauty and mesmerized King Solomon.

Guinevere

was the Queen consort of King Arthur. One of the most prominent story arcs is her love affair with Arthur's chief knight Sir Lancelot.

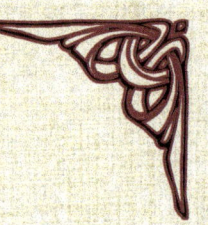

Berenice of Cilicia

was a Jewish client queen of the Roman Empire during the second half of the 1st century. She was the daughter of King Herod Agrippa I and a sister of King Herod Agrippa II.

Esther

was a Jewish queen of the Persian king Ahasuerus. Ahasuerus is traditionally identified with Xerxes I during the time of the Achaemenid empire.

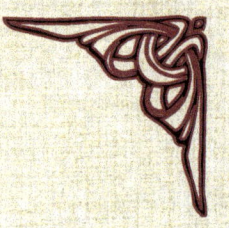

Salome

was the daughter of Herod II and Herodias. The story goes that she agreed to perform a dance in exchange for the head of John the Baptist.

Eleanor of Aquitaine

was one of the wealthiest and most powerful women in western Europe during the High Middle Ages. She became Duchess of Aquitaine in her own right while she was still a child.

Agnes Sorel

was a favourite mistress of King Charles VII of France. She is considered the first officially recognized royal mistress.

Catherine the Great

was the most renowned and the longest-ruling female leader of Russia. Russia was revitalized under her reign, growing larger and stronger than ever and becoming recognized as one of the great powers of Europe.

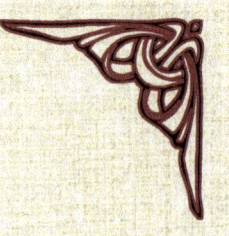

Lillie Langtry

was celebrated as a young woman of beauty and charm, who later established a reputation as an actress and producer. By 1881, she had become an actress and starred in many plays.

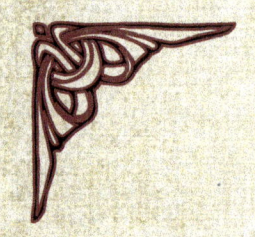

Marilyn Monroe

was an American actress, model, and singer, starring in a number of commercially successful motion pictures during the 1950s and early 1960s.

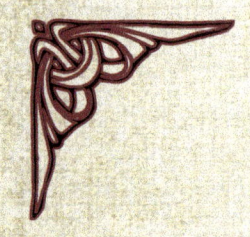

Audrey Hepburn

was a British actress. epburn was active during Hollywood's Golden Age. She is regarded by some to be the most naturally beautiful woman of all time.

Lightning Source UK Ltd.
Milton Keynes UK
UKHW051252091222
413667UK00010B/325